CHANNEL

BARNARD

NEW

WOMEN

POETS   1986

SERIES   *Heredity*

. . .   PATRICIA STORACE

Edited by

Christopher   1987

Baswell   *Laughing at Gravity: Conversations*
                         with Isaac Newton

and
                         ELIZABETH SOCOLOW

Celeste

Schenck   1988

                         The World, the Flesh, and Angels

                         MARY B. CAMPBELL

Barbara Jordan

CHANNEL

With an

Introduction

by

Molly

Peacock

BEACON PRESS

BOSTON

Beacon Press
25 Beacon Street
Boston, Massachusetts 02108-2892
www.beacon.org

Beacon Press books
are published under the auspices of
the Unitarian Universalist Association of Congregations.

First digital-print edition 2001

Portions of this work have appeared in the following publications:
Boulevard: "Web, "Orion"; The New Criterion: "To England"; Sulfur: "Collecting the
Elements" under the title "Branching"; Boston Literary Review: "Cupid, Death, and the
Beyond"; Zone: A Feminist Journal for Women and Men: "The Cannibals of Autumn";
Ironwood: four sections from "Tutelary Poems"; Anima: "Thunderhead," "Poem for German
Painters," "Titan Myth," "Channel"; Wind: "an Act of Faith"; Giants Play Well in the Drizzle:
"Walpurgisnacht"; Grolier Prize Anthology, 1985: "Ode," "Philosopher's Walk, Heidelberg,"
"Channel," "Poem for German Painters"; Art Zone: "We All Have Many Chances"; Passage
North: "Poem" ("A reptilian sheen . . ."); The International Poetry Review: "Real Places";
Yankee Magazine: "Genesis."

Library of Congress Cataloging-in-Publication Data
Jordan, Barbara.
Channel / Barbara Jordan ; with an introduction by Molly Peacock.
p.   cm. — (Barnard new women poets series)
isbn 0-8070-6808-X. — isbn 0-8070-6809-8 (pbk.)
I. Title. II. Series.
ps3560.067c4   1990
811´.54—dc20   89-43074

For my husband, Edward Batchelder

CONTENTS

ACKNOWLEDGMENTS

I ESPECIALLY WISH TO THANK MY FRIEND GERALD Burns, whose poetry should be more widely read, for his delightful erudition and the pleasure of his recommended reading lists. Over the past two years, as we conversed and traded poems and books, my work took new shape, influenced in great measure by the discussions we had and the curious mirror they became.

I also want to thank the Massachusetts Artists Foundation and the Ellen LaForge Memorial Poetry Foundation, Inc., for their awards, and, most importantly, I wish to thank Barnard College for their New Women Poets Series, which made this book possible.

INTRODUCTION

Molly Peacock

IF PRAYER MUST HAVE AN OBJECT, THEN PER-
haps its richest object is understanding. The process of
prayer involves an extreme awareness of the self, so aware
as to see at last the self's limitations, and so aware of *these*
as to crave connection with the outer world, as a kind of
completion. In *Channel,* Barbara Jordan's poems seem to
engage in this process quite informally, but so intensely
that I can't help thinking of her sumptuous first book as a
series of acts of prayer, as if she has written a highly per-
sonal (and therefore quite idiosyncratic) and highly intel-
ligent (and therefore quite challenging) book of hours.
Each poem in *Channel* becomes a channel through expe-
rience to understanding.

There is another way that *Channel* reminds me of a
book of hours: it is richly illustrative, filled with visual
material so dense, and phrasing so intense, that one could
be wandering through medieval forests of illumination.
This visual and linguistic energy seems both to comprise
the text and to surround it, sometimes appearing to ob-
scure meaning, until one adjusts to the richness. It comes
as no surprise that Barbara Jordan once attended art
school. Her vision is muscular; she does not so much
watch (as poet-observers often do) as much as she *sees* in
the physically connected way that painters often see. In
the "Tutelary Poems" she gives us a visual quotation:

> —for Anselm Kiefer

> The Rhine's smudged silhouette, pink ichor
>   of sunset,
> is dragged across the canvas
> like a sacrifice.

The lushness of her imagery, from leopards to tourmalines, creates "an enchantment of peripheries," as she tells us in "Shell Pond Woods." This imagery, which is evoked by equally luscious vocabulary, displays itself in precisely crafted, almost graphically designed poems, even down to the juxtaposition of lines, and the conscious spacing of words to occur *under* other words, fostering intricate phrase relations. Although their verbal gestures are not similar, Jordan recalls Marianne Moore in the passion of her poetic construction. Note that "of sunset" is intentionally placed. "It is not that the line runs on too long," Barbara Jordan has explained to me, "but that I want those words exactly there."

So understanding really is at issue here. Jordan struggles to understand the world, creating an aesthetic out of her attempts. Her vocabulary, both quite wild and quite precise, creates an intensified surface to the poems, and it helps to think of this surface like the built-up surface of a painting. She makes what I would call a "textured text." "You cannot use a word without being aware of its secondary usages. Almost like a painter, a poet can 'bring out' hidden connotations through the surrounding language," Barbara Jordan says in a statement about her book. Readers will find abundant examples of this, but one of the more apparent ones occurs in "Web":

> Language is what we feed on, feeling each "vowel's
>   velvet,"
> an interrogation of atmosphere.

This interrogation, a gentle, persistent questioning of all things, becomes her quest. "O God," she says in "Collecting the Elements,"

> . . . who are the tunnel in which we walk,
> all things express a thought that was not ours before
> we seized it from the air, the forest floor.

Her questionings that are her quest combine with her "textured text" to create an aesthetic of awe. It may not be easy for the reader of the often quite accessible stock of American first books of poetry to know quite what to make of her. I didn't, at first. I don't think I read *Channel* so much as circled it, feeling a bit like Frances Hodgson Burnett's character Mary looking for the entrance to the Secret Garden. If you remember the book, perhaps you will recall that the garden was absolutely worth the determination one had to muster to find the entrance.

For Jordan, language *itself* is searched for its entrance points. In a statement about her work she says, "It is a particular challenge to take a word that has been eroded, as it were, through too much handling—like 'beauty' or 'truth'—and attempt to evoke new freshness from it." In the title poem, "Channel," Jordan resuscitates a dead word for a living idea:

> It is only the word that's dead;
> the serpentine *g*, the dogged *d*, surround
>   the *o*
> without animism: a drainpipe
> opening into a field under a highway.

Of course the word she breathes life into is what has breathed life into her. The god she unearths is the source of all vocabulary. The poem continues:

> Sometimes for centuries
> a word will disappear into its meaning
> to return transfigured,
> arcane; and the whole language
> alters.

For a word to disappear into its own meaning: the offbeat accuracy of the idea is characteristic of Jordan. "When ideas get weary," she says in "Web," "you fan them / with beautiful concentration." Her preoccupation with meaning, vocabulary, and texture reminds me of Geoffrey Hill, a writer Jordan admires. In Hill's work, words become the viscera of imagery, as they do in her "Tutelary Poems":

> The woods clutched in sweet smells recede
> into carnality, the murmurous daybeds of mantis
>   and blue-bead lily.
> A hawk stabs what he has vomited,
> confirms the thing is dead before he lets it
> fall.

Jordan often expresses a horrified sympathy with the natural world, for it is both a place where she feels most herself, and a place where she may externalize the enactment of the self's conflicts. The peacock-eating leopards of "The Discovery Room," the opening poem of the collection, are a shocking case in point. The natural world is not where her questions are answered so much as displayed, as they are in "Orion."

> I resume my petty squabbles with fate,
> its patient and subversive tongue; configurations
> of loneliness; stars
> rattling in a box.

Though they are schooled and intelligent and aware of culture, especially in their range of historical and anthropological references (look at poems such as "'A Skull Enwalled Garden,'" "Tropism," or "Titan Myth"), they *still* seem to come out of nowhere. Perhaps that is because Barbara Jordan herself comes out of nowhere, having pursued for many years an independent path. She attended art school, married, and worked as a secretary while slowly developing herself as a writer. It is only in the past few years that she has studied full time at Boston University and led a life more connected to her writing. Here we have the result of the deeply interior processing that goes on when a poet must compartmentalize her art, write "on the side," so to speak. What happens with someone as gifted as Barbara

Jordan is that what society has shifted "to the side" of her life is just what she has focused on most intently. In her "Tutelary Poems" she says,

> We are the wishing wells
> of God, we are the pods of grace,
> encumbered by the pretext
> of everlasting life

I can imagine the wishing well that sustained her through years of typing and answering phones. Having led what seemed a double life, she has chronicled the interior one. She is a poet who has spent a great deal of time inside her own head and who has the courage to paint what is in her own mind. "Art is an expression," she reminds us in her poem "Vespers," "as prayer." I think what she means by this is what Kafka may have meant when he said that writing is a form of prayer; prayer reaches toward understanding through the expression of true feelings and thoughts. As such, it is an expressive act, and so, of course, is writing— though writing is not only expressive, it is creative, and it generates its own world, complete. The degree of completeness of that world creates beauty, while expression addresses truth. But it is always a joyful relief to one faced with explaining a writer's work when the writer herself offers the clearest comment. Here is how Jordan has responded to some of my ideas about her book:

While I do not regard my poems specifically as prayers, I do try to discover language "doors" through which to approach the sacred; most of my poems are engendered by a sense of awe. For me, it is always the ineffable which demands expression. Each poem is a channel through which I attempt to bring something I understand on a preconscious level into a more concrete clarity. The poem reinforces and refracts a central act of knowing: it points. In this way, it is a kind of path.

To our enlightenment, I might add.

I

THE DISCOVERY ROOM

THE DISCOVERY ROOM

Two leopards have eaten a peacock.
Their habitat is a ravine strewn with the bird's
                    feathers,
sheltered by trees, crepuscular.
A second bird escapes into a painted forest,
smell of cedar.
The leopards are used to death, already
they have looked away from it:
one rests a paw upon the remains,
lightly, as St. Jerome might signify a skull
            on the writing desk;
his eyes hold a menacing frankness.

A small boy crosses the room, drawn to them.
"What have they done?" he shrieks, his face pressed
            at the glass.
"They've killed a peacock," his parents say.
"Why?"
"To eat it."
"Oh, my GOD," he whispers, tiny jaw a rictus,
comprehending; omnivorous;
waist-high. His parents smile at us.

ORION

Emissaries come from the pond—a red-winged
blackbird and a dog. Nothing else
yet. The silence is magnetic.

Several days, at dusk,
I've hoped to see a moose. I'm told they appear
where the pine forest stands
half-submerged. Its shadows are turning
articulate, claiming whole regions.

These are the minutes of gauze. Sky and water meet
and spore; follicles open in midair.

On the far shore, a rack of black branches
becomes the vortex of expectancy—if it should lift,
from lapping, its animal's head out of darkness
with eyes gleaming.

I resume my petty squabbles with fate,
its patient and subversive tongue; configurations
of loneliness; stars
rattling in a box.

COLLECTING THE ELEMENTS

> Rarity, strangeness, and beauty have in
> them an inexplicable element, and the
> inexplicable is always potentially magical.
>
> —Joan Evans, *Magical Jewels*

At the pool bottom green jasper, tourmaline, amber,
som tymes the very Images of the Starres naturally ingrafted
                              in them,
and others in their perspicuity like water
congealed in sunset's red extravagance;
and he 't hath it in his keeping it will sure preserve him.
I make my hand a spathe to cup the stones
where timelessness hangs in quicksands of cold
and leaves. I tilt my chin to sniff the air,
an animal comforted by privacy
beneath uddered, monumental clouds; choosing this or that
by instinct. The Saxon peasant tilling fields mistook
arrow-heads for snakes' tongues, petrified
venom as a talisman. How to define magick? The letter z
                              is its salt
in spell words whispered from Byzantium,
the glossopetra of demons: wind-blown, unearthed among
                              beetroot.

In a garden in Cologne, in a stork's nest, Avicenna
found an "eaglestone"—a cure for childbirth—the place
                              pertinent.
O God, who are the tunnel in which we walk,
all things express a thought that was not ours before
we seized it from the air, the forest floor.
Bacon once swallowed crushed pearls and lemon juice
as good for bones.
Vapors seep from earth, the dusk explores its issues in
                              the grass,
and matter forms conspiringly as if it had a will.

Along a path to the Manor House at Tunbridge Wells,
                              badgers had dug
their mounds under the fan tracery of ancient shrubs
and made it ominous, for the walk veered into dank
sound chambers, the birthing rooms
of wary creatures. Shall we *sêc lytle stones* in the maw
                              of young swallows—
en swealwan bridda magan?
The air smells of sphagnum moss and fear, the sun
moves in the leaves like a diamond-back.
One wants to pull back fear just to watch the glistening
                              pupae
being carried, a small reflection of anxieties.

A hush sheds over claw and branch,
over speech. The trees make paths too, can mesmerize you
                          with a life's work,
a propendency that beckons up
through scalar coolness, shadows you hack way
to sky—observing leaf-clusters, the texture of a bole—
                                    any opening
a foothold to get *under* the diadem
in place to listen. Droplet sounds. Insects buffeting
the curved skin of wood. A neolithic woman
put the forest around her neck: a necklace strung
                    of fifty teeth—
three of lion, the rest of bear—
to hoard, to stitch into a hem of rain, to make
a voice that did not lie.

"A SKULL ENWALLED GARDEN"

—from "Visions of the Fathers of Lascaux"
by Clayton Eshleman

When, in the evening, I explore the succulent shadows
with their blue veins and black chrysanthemums,
their thorny places,
and the galaxy of milk that life is—then what I am
and am not
falls away. When I open the dictionary,
there is a beetle which lays its eggs
on the bodies of mice and birds
before it buries them. Again and again, the page where
it lives
falls open. The etching is nineteenth century,
crosshatched, the beetle studiously digging a hole,
the rodent nearby, on its back, feet curled.

When I was twelve, I found *Gods, Graves, & Scholars*
in the library.
I don't know why I took it down,
but I saw—isolated as if for surgery—the unwrapped
Head of Tutankhamen,
the blighted face. His empty eye sockets were more
distant
than all the winter stars when I took out the trash
and looked until my neck ached.

Something in the bushes would rustle and scare me,
because a soul is full of windy spaces,
but I thought that nothing could get in unless I let it
                                        willingly.
Once from an upstairs window, I stood dazed
watching the Aurora Borealis—rare at that latitude—
churn the nightsky like a quartz fish-mud;

What for these strange facts remembered? Melon seeds
                            in the stomach
of a Chinese princess, dead 2,000 years. This page
a sack of warm wind, and cloud-swamped avenues
                            and trees
that hold up the sky dorically;
while to sit on, the kind of tufted grass I like.

BRUEGEL'S CROWS

High in bare trees, high above trampled snow,
Bruegel's crows observe.

Each prefers a different branch
and view.
They straddle a bit of wind; they strain and coextend
        like stamens
of a black, invisible flower.
Their grace is retrograde, is time-released.

What if they are emissaries of an impersonal God?

What if nothing is watching?
Or only us.
We see a sixteenth-century town, its tiny skaters
        and sturdy bridge;
our eyes, too, are calipers—
measuring menace in a white world.

POEM FOR GERMAN PAINTERS

I will paint my God
bigger than anything else on the canvas.

My God swells up
to fill the space you give him.

The lungs of my God
are two Gothic cathedrals.

My God is the smoke
blowing across the plain.

I will paint my God
as a precocious child
nursing on marble.

I will paint my God
with muscles of linden
and a back decayed by the world.

I will paint my God suffering,
because he suffers more
than your God.

His tears drown the peasants
who live along the Oder River.

THE CANNIBALS OF AUTUMN

Neither time's worn edges, nor violent windows
    (climbed by trickling leaves)
recall a race
that possessed no contour apart from landscape,
but just as we, if we lived roofless,
would be oppressed by an orchard darkness
upon ourselves and our appliances.
          And the strangled wisteria,
vagrant at the back door, autumn after autumn
as we grow suspicious, cling to our reflections
like lizards of prayer.

I've walked through the city of gargoyles, Paris,
where drops and torrents
erode those prolonged mouths, the way blood is
    wished for in words.
What surprise is it, then, that sounds
catch in basins
on windy days that shake all contemplation
blowing boxes on the water.

WEB

Not pretext, but cut branches and then weeds
make a *faux* wilderness, conceal the snare.
Amethyst, opal, bullfrog, thorn—
how words entice us! Lovely, substantive,
who would think the floor could drop? An empty
        cage is poignant:
iron ones from the Inquisition
seen now, without tenants, keep elusive
horror. Nothing will poke through this paper,
not dry bones, not woods. When ideas get weary
        you fan them
with beautiful concentration,
the way dragonflies hover near water.
Language is what we feed on, feeling each "vowel's
        velvet,"
an interrogation of atmosphere.

Perhaps the world is still; the mood won't be coaxed—
as mallard herl and wool wrapped in hair
may interest a trout.
Skill is subordinate to chance, the promiscuity
        of chance.
The spider lays a web in shade, suspends itself
across a hedge; and we regard it
with mild attention—like an aquarium skull
        that fish swim through—
bending down to look at
what's been caught.

SHELL POND WOODS

They hear us before we break cover
into the square summer field,
and the hot whir of cicadas and honeybees
drowns any rustling at the edge
where deer and hare and fox have fled
to wait concealed by leaves—
like creatures in the borders of an illumined
     manuscript.
How many times we've held our breath
into this clearing, anticipating an impossible
     Eden
of night predators basking in sun,
of a bear mesmerized by an apple tree.
Yet always, the plain text is comforting:
daisies and meadow grass, exclamations
at the random monarch.
"Next time," we say, and homeward
sense the enchantment of peripheries;
the furtive reappearances.

REAL PLACES

That morning we took a path in the woods above
                    the orchards
until we found a wall
and a patio broken by weeds and twisted vines.
Impelled by romance,
we climbed to a mooring on the hill: four chimneys
and a bannister.
Sometime in the 1920s it burned, the pines also,
and what grew in the urns before moss.
Only a towering oak paddled the sky
like the gatesman
exhorting the guests to escape.

~   ~   ~

Fists of skunk cabbage rise under leafy helmets,
the irises fly;

I don't like to look in the well, and see my face
in its predatory eye.

~   ~   ~

"What beast lives there?" my father asked.
No beast, it was a child's nest.

At five I ran away from home
with a loaf of bread and tea bags and a cup.

The frog shadow of the house
lengthened on the lawn; from behind the forsythia
I watched my mother
flap and pin the wash and go inside.
"Good-bye," she'd called.

~   ~   ~

The trees twist suddenly,
the wind claps the moths to the screen.
A woman stands on a porch
amid an eyewash of greenery, a latticework
of dripping leaves, sounds
from many levels.

Remoteness and the humid air intoxicate.
I know the nostalgia, the incantations of these
                              afternoons
when I'm a stranger in my own rooms
and the things I'm fond of
reflect nothing that I am.

~   ~   ~

Whose breath's against the screen at sunset?
A child's.

And who's in for good tonight?
A longing that transcends the next time.

Beyond the window, fields beget fields
where the years go like great swan dives.
We run after them,
trampling the ferns and grasses, looking upward,
as if time
were a stone you could rub.

GENESIS

Far from the sea, the lilies grow
and listen for the sea.

Long ago, they bloomed near the shore,
and the small crustaceans,
red-backed crabs,
scurried under the pale exotic plants
that rocked on thin stems
half-flower, half-shell.

It's a long way from the beginning.

The heavenly beasts appear in the sky,
unchanged
since the first seeds fell on the fields
in a green rain,
and men climbed from the water
on two legs,
unsteady as baby goats.

In the wind now
the white flowers rise and bend
in the grass, like the heads of sheep.
Behind the mountains
the waves rise and fall. The stars open.

No one has left the garden.

EARLY EVENING

The trees oust their birds
into a blowing, lilac sky
and the perpendicular flocks disperse
to mythology.

But on this branch, a grackle trills
to the chameleon hour,
throws back his neck, and ripples
                          his throat
like a columbine.

PERSPECTIVE

Nothing in the wind
but rumors among pigeons,
and a scrap of paper lifted over the roofs
like the soul of a tomcat.

On the horizon the roofs are on fire,
the sunlight ricochets
off the hills.
My body seems huge, and everything possible,
as I stand on a balcony

amazed as a sailor who climbs the mast,
and seeing the plenitude of the sea,
can't choose
where to cast the net,
but clings to the rigging,
his hair blown back like a kingfisher's.

AN ACT OF FAITH

In the water I see stars, among the reeds
the mountain of my face,
and across a distance two geese
in the twilight of a lake, like stilettos.
So many touchstones. I lean toward life,
I unbuckle the flowers' roots,
hold birds
and know the privilege, know the trees
as vessels of shadow.

And if the sky is gray and anguished gray
                         above a field
before a storm—
and the leaves shake, shake, shake
with a spiritual palsy—
I look over my shoulder unsure: am I observed,
or do I observe?

Let show all things splendid,
in their darker nature
splendid also. Lord, you know the mask
of my face, how I peer at the world
from under a leaf, from under the squint
of my intelligence.

I can't comprehend, or find contradiction
in evidence of past millenniums, the broken
ancient skulls,
galaxies behind the sun. Certainly all creatures
pause, and gaze benignly
into the air, into the light where birds fly
                         and are gone:
this is the Light I lean toward.

II

TUTELARY POEMS

I

All my steps are thresholds.
I walk on blue rocks,
the same watery, unreal blue
that Fra Angelico mixed to hold the Virgin
      to her bier,
levitating, like a magician's assistant,
pumped full of sky.

Early, I set the bowl of milk on a stone
for the serpent
with his dropdead eyes, with his mercurial
methodology.
     The green phalanxes of the forest
lift their leaves when the wind shifts,
in unison,
as if to show me their weapons.

III

All things become sacred from long gazing.
The weedy, ancient Roman floor
carries the weight of stars
in its prehensile pool;
and overnight, the glass left on the porch
        fills with awe.
Every year we say we think that spring
will never come,
then the hyacinth pours out its fragrances,
and time transforms
my staring at the sky.

IV

Rain fragments upon the protective leaves,
upon the perplexed stamen face,
the planetesimal rustling.
Votive flower,
the day has let out its dogs, and clouds
        are riveted to the land.
There is treason on the hidden stair
that goes down into the roots
where the god sits.

V

—for Anselm Kiefer

The Rhine's smudged silhouette, pink ichor
          of sunset,
is dragged across the canvas
like a sacrifice. The upheaved birds
ignite their wings,
extinguish in the garnet wood.
We come to probe a bowl of blood, to stare
          into the pit
begotten by a toppled oak.

V I

The woods clutched in sweet smells recede
into carnality, the murmurous daybeds of mantis
      and blue-bead lily.
A hawk stabs what he has vomited,
confirms the thing is dead before he lets it
fall.
We communicate on human terms: toss his claw
      on a divination board
with a baboon's tooth, a 1929 Dutch coin,
and read the storms we've shaken from a jar.

VII

Summer evening, and a miasma of gnats
whirls under the lilacs.
The landscape takes on a dashboard glow.
I cross small bridges
of light; I wander inside a grave rubbing
        where textures deceive.
The lilies resolve
into mortar and pistil.
Lamps go out in the scattered stones.

VIII

To see a room,
not through a keyhole, but through a key
found at dusk:
magic that will fit the verdigrised lock, open
        the cabinet of ghosts
when the field is empty
(a fossil of moth's wing on shale)
and each lone firefly is beckoning, like an X
upon a map.

I X

Medicine box with design of crows in a forest
17th century, gold on black lacquer,
quiets me
like watching snow from under a bridge.
        All objects are clocks.
I breathe on the vertebrate mirror, the hushed
confessional
filled with the lineage of twilight:
summers fray into winters, everything flies
        away.
Sometimes, I daydream catastrophe.

X

Light drains from the sky, and the streetlights
insinuate a row of martinis;
the trees step back into passageways.
Difficult to distinguish
the portents of evil from an east wind
      off the river.
A drink is a flame I carry upstairs:
autumn, and blood near the surface of things.

X I

The world dismantles. November's sacrificial matters
have befallen: scraps in an empty lion's cage,
a laminous cold.
The clouds are very high, and *above* more peripheral
        than *over,*
where a hive distills a single bee, then shuts
the cover on the sky.
I am unwieldy with prayer,
and concoct a wistfulness that will not burn.

XII

A cawing in the wind, inarticulate
because
it's dim now; it can't be traced. Sunset inclines
        the spires, and moodiness
pollutes my plans. We are the wishing wells
of God, we are the pods of grace,
encumbered by the pretext
of everlasting life.

III

CHANNEL

CHANNEL

It is only the word that's dead;
the serpentine *g*, the dogged *d*, surround
      the *o*
without animism: a drainpipe
opening into a field under a highway.

Compare the verdure of *paganism*
(*a*'s are always green, and *pale* is green,
      pond also),
a word that rises on its haunches—
a meadow with birds.
Even *atheist*, scaffolded on metaphysics,
oxidizes into air
like a great cathedral returning to the
      mineral kingdom.
But *god* is hanging from a limb, a lens
focused between the sky
and soul,
a cipher to be warmed or cooled.

Sometimes for centuries
a word will disappear into its meaning
to return transfigured,
arcane; and the whole language
alters.

POEM

A reptilian sheen in the sky,
a predatory darkness
wincing with stars. In this cup of creation
the wind descends
and lifts the trees, lifts my heart
and the tiny hairs between my shoulders
in a blowing fire. I will give my life
for this love that boomerangs light-years;
I will walk to the edge
and memorize the sky.

What I fear is the wilderness:
not the earth's,
but the spirit's wilderness,
where there are abandonments beyond description.

I remember the beautiful dilemma
on the mountain, the compulsion to fly
over the valley,
the exigency that held me
and left me subdued. What shall we believe
beyond the natural law?

The earth is bread we take and eat.

TITAN MYTH

For the pensive God
Hates
Untimely growth
                    —Hölderlin

Recorded time, by flora embellished, and by
        stars pacified
to symbol and the drooping branches
of language, is but a little epoch
that has made the heavens heavy.

This moment is anchored: a day
with a humid hush, the pines stirring
        pollen;
and I am Reason amidst the hydrangeas
examining the deep blue flowers.

500,000,000 years ago
the world was a wilderness of Ordovician
mosses, the sky was patient—
or perhaps clouds like phantom dinosaurs
        stalked the horizon,
feeding on rain
for their parthenogenesis.

We have their bones, extinct before light
fell on new metal: the eyes
of Babygod, awake
in love with a ceiling indistinguishable
        from existence,
this brain curled like a white serpent
in the skull's firmament.

Gods, giants, nimble-footed dryads—
the anxieties of an age
breed their own propaganda. Like choosing
one's favorite insect
there is fascination with the fuselage,
horror at the mandibles—and only man
        can put wings
on the lion, make him guard the gates
to Babylon.

If I knew the precise hour of my flowering,
        I could give up
the sidelong glances at the sky,
as if some force delayed my ripeness,
        left me here
in this garden,
surrounded by the knowledge of names:
lilies and *oaks, the Holy Spirit.*

Returning across the grass at sunset, the
      shadows of trees
resurrect the primordial beasts,
make me think of Hesiod's lost work
on bird divination,
the streets of history, the patient deity.

And Socrates, with your steep hemlock,
in the blue lip of a lake
the day is turning to fire.

AIRPLANE

In the twilight, an airplane solemnifies
              the tranquil sky.
We breathe moss cocktails that a breeze fills,
and follow its arc—the way a frog observes
              a remote firefly,
inhales the vanity of landscape.

Where do our lives empty
as we walk on balconies?
The lakes of Botticelli blue deepen behind
              the tiny light,
imprint it on eyes
eclipsed by trees.

The stellar beauty of the age required a mirror
and people on lawnchairs
instinctively threw their hearts into space.
The conversations turned to the enemies'
              arsenals,
the christening of missiles.

THUNDERHEAD

Outside of me an oracle gathered,
from childhood building what it kept. It was
                an undertow
that vanished memories under its weight,
a storm for me to climb.

Each day begins, the will to change assumed;
this sky obliterates the others.
Yet life exists
in a deciduous light: a green roof
over the years, obscuring the path of crumbs
our dreams leave into the woods. All that is
                unremembered
exists, perhaps, on the wild side of death,
among ruins and golden formulas
to hold us accountable.

Here, granite stairs divide a hill,
and end in timelessness, and daffodils.

Forgiveness: a simple bandage.
This morning the sky is a manageable blue,
I hold my life to my mouth
and take it in my arms, saying nothing.
Through the window the trees change dimension
                              while I stare,
and a bird enters a corridor and disappears,
like a glove lost from a bridge.

The wind pitched hard
that day in the orchards; I flew to breathe it.
In the palm of the hill
stones pushed from the ground like molars, or
              the worn hooves of Clydesdales
uncovered from long-ago harvests.
Hornets dragged over apples, and I sat,
              for the grass grew in my joints
and I began to cry.
What will I become in this place?

I'm afraid of a wasted life, to find myself
the face behind a curtain
in an upstairs room, a dispassionate woman
watching shadows cross the lawn
and black spoons lifting among the leaves
in the evening.

WALL PAINTING

My deity lives in an empty frame, 3½' by 4½',
through which I see a nightsky
and no alien life.

The motif of the garden pool
opened windows in Egyptian tombs: ducks paddled
                        among the lotus,
fish and insects wedged
in eternity.

In sadness
I am standing in cold water. Anselm Kiefer's
                        charred pond light,
gutted room
entitled "To the Supreme Being."

But black dilutes. The sky recomposes
from washed sapphire to ash
clouding the same arch. This widens and closes
  with wind,
an elm's retractable talons;
while below, four startled crows branch off—
  leaving their voices,
a meal half-eaten they'll resume.

The rain collected in a tree stump has slackened
  to silvery scum,
a mirror clouded with insects' wings,
their small deaths providential, and moody
  in decay;
damp moss gives off a whiff of Hecate.
I wanted a chemistry set because of loving
the woods, to own bottles tinctured with green
  remedies, and poisons
as purple as Borgias.
Today, a strong wind siphons the past,

and spring and summer touch me as ghosts.
Nothing keeps. In the shag rugs of autumn,
I lay down my carapace,
and feel the slow secretion of anger, a tunnel
  opening
under my ribs—sky of archangel blue.
The throaty caw of birds
shakes somewhere in the long grass, thickly,
  like thistles.

CUPID, DEATH, AND THE BEYOND

—After an etching by Max Klinger

I believe in the innocence of the future,
as Klinger saw it: a Roman lake shored by the sky
        and a row of trees,
invaded by a child and a skeleton.
Behind them, more like a ligament, the ghostcloud
of life's provisions—
amazing how far I push
to escape that forest in a closet,
deny everything but a frontal attack on a mirage.

There are days that rush on wheels
to a destination,
shattering each wall of air; impetuous—
until one encapsulated moment spins me around
        in the space of a breath,
and I long for the loneliness of an opponent.

VESPERS

The trees live various postures, their shade
falls across the hedges at sunset.
I feel the clarity of the light, the soberness
of the hour
when the day is over and memorized.

This tigerlily is benign as a child's finger,
a channel to the sinuous earth
where the dead feed the timeless placenta;
it rises
like a beautiful bird I may touch—
and a conversation passes between us,
although it only listens.

I accept the boundary of death, the fixed grave
above which the stars repeat
their configurations. Here is the life-mark,
the chart says,
and here is the death-mark.
I look into the window of the flower
and admire its passion;
I think of the lunar markings of the moths,
and the saprophytic Indian-pipe
that comes forth
in paleness, more the imaginary flora of a star.

Each is what it is: an expression,
as art is an expression,
as prayer.

WALPURGISNACHT

> Indeed, it is the worst grief not to know why . . .
> —Verlaine

Grayer than a dog whistle Verlaine's verse
echoes through mist and the laburnum,
attending this world like moss on a skyscraper.

A misanthropic wind collects us
in his pasture of statues, rubbing our eyes
at the somnambulism of poetry.

He tortured his gaze on shadows, twisted
the leaves backwards from dawn.
Thoughts, shaken from trees in his midnight
         topiary,
fall into water, like dominoes,
or move as a breeze across the grass.

At 4 A.M. it can happen, to see crows
meet in a circle. Or dream the atavistic bird,
         human-sized,
running away from the light.
But we awaken, drenched in the partial bronze
of the will,

and we've slept, no doubt, suffering the exorcism
of names and places,
bittersweet as spring, and the green absinthe.

PHILOSOPHER'S WALK, HEIDELBERG

Birds wafted in the mechanical walls
            of the Schloss,
and in the locked gardens
slanting away from the Neckar,
up all those steps.
Wasn't it like making the Stations of the Cross
            through Germany—
remembering the millions dead, and we living
staring at the sky as if it were the last sip
                        in a cup?

At sunset,
we followed down Hölderlin Way, immersed
            in wrought-iron gates
overgrown with grape leaves,
and the mute keyholes of ownership lost. It was
            an old path
for hecatombs. Birds leapfrogged their mates.
The light snagged us
in a web, where the gods of Greece obscured
                        the Hapsburgs.

For an hour we vanished
inside the velvet drapery of the past—to pull
            a bellrope
and have the present summoned.
Life is a wall among ruins. And it seemed, on
            the opposite hill,
that the castle turrets echoed our meditations.
We were poets and in love.
Then, like a branch caught by a current, the sun
            darkened, and sank.

TO ENGLAND

A world was lined in velvet. Its garden pillars
                    like huge chrysalides
trailed off into the unkempt
woods of fox dens and tungsten skies;
and its emblems—honeybees sealed in glass
           and pronged into rings,
halls of padded rodents and hummingbirds—
made nature less a precipice,
her exits and entrances as lifesize as a wish.

Kingdom of backyard naturalists,
cartographer of sacred stones.
Once, your aristocracy had a periscope in every
                    chimney,
and wore, to hunt, the Order of the Stoat on
                    their lapels;
Thumbelina floated in a walnut shell,
and dioramas of The Great Fire and Waterloo
preserved, like a plague arm in formaldehyde.

ALL OF ONE MIND

In a Dark Age, clergy and congregation crossed a field
to a hollow stump. A man spoke,
there to excommunicate a swarm of bees for murder:
"Let them be dissipated like smoke."
Others answered, "As wax flows before fire, let sinners
          perish before God,"
and lit the torch.

Today, against white sky, blackbirds descend in a long
          ermine cloak
upon an elm, solemnly, as if that settlement
were permanent. But nothing is; mercurial, they scatter,
all of one mind
into the darker quadrants of the rain.

In the cemetery where I walk—it is
a park—past rushes and willows, beside a pond choked
          with dull reflections,
I see the bees returning to the crypts
that house their hives. By circumventing iron grids,
          and fleur-de-lis and lily spokes,
they enter through the doors like ordinary guests—
though few come.
Intrusion is an art, the way thorns and berries
          creep into heraldry
to suggest a forest; or trees converge upon a path,
seed the grave's slate stone.

Placidia, Queen of the Goths, sat for centuries
          in her mausoleum
visible through a chink in the wall,
before children, dabbling with fire, burned throne
and corpse.

"Firm stanzas hang," Stevens wrote, "like hives
          in hell";
mine are not so adamant, for things escape,
and light and dark cross-pollinate.
The sun comes up
brilliant upon the waters and swaying azaleas.
          Bees drone
back and forth, from the crypts to the flowers.

TROPISM

Jung on Mt. Elgon, Thompson at Chichén-Itzá,
solitary with the whole jungle behold the aqueduct
        of dawn
across the disclosed boulders, affiliations
of vines. No sound, only the spread of light—
level, eventual,
in a moment like tea steeping.

From his seat under an acacia tree in the semi-
        darkness,
Jung saw baboons assemble, each daybreak,
on the ridge of the cliff.
"Like me, they seemed to be waiting for sunrise,"
        he wrote,
& recognized the living pillars of Abu Simbel,
an old hunger on the watchtower.

When Thompson found the Sacred Well
the surface was obsidian smooth, clogged with brown-
        green algae,
with rotting vegetation: a pool 187 feet across,
80 deep. Into this, from a rock on which the priest
        had stood,
he threw logs carved to resemble women—
deciding where to dredge.

First tons of wet muck.
The bones of a jaguar and a deer brought up together,
                         "evidence
of a forest tragedy"; then lumps of copal·incense,
a human skull.

In my dream it was under a rosebush led there, down
                         the hidden stair
to a chamber. It was silence I found,
and a blue light
older than dawn. Everything I've done falls
                         into it,
the way stars fade at daybreak.

1486

—for Harlen Welsh

On such a day of gold and blue,
Pico della Mirandola must have walked
        in his garden,
calling the angels to his wrist, the true
God's falconer.

What wonder to gaze out
at the world within, knowing it was the same
diorama of clouds and fragrances,
the pious woods, and chrysolite reflecting
        pools.
Echoes and images
concatenate a wise man to his Love;

His soul becomes the crucible,
and prayer, the incantations of his art.
And if it rained beyond his joy,
        the center held.
From opulence and candlelight,
whispers of the sacred name
embarked on predatory flights
to snare the bloodless forces down.

NOTES ON POEMS

COLLECTING THE ELEMENTS, PAGE 5: While reading *Magical Jewels of the Middle Ages and the Renaissance* by Joan Evans (1922; reprint, New York: Dover Publications, 1976), I was struck by the peculiar logic which governs magical beliefs—specifically, how ancient arrowheads, uncovered in tilled fields, were used as talismans. In shape, they resembled snakes' tongues, and were thought to be petrified, or "stone tongues" (glossopetra). Because some snakes are poisonous, these objects were assumed to have the power to detect poison. Interestingly, the arrowheads were set in gold and precious gems and mounted on the dinner plates of the nobility. (If water condensed on the talisman, the food was poisonous.)

Italicized sections of "Collecting the Elements" are also quoted from *Magical Jewels,* which attributes "and 't who hath it in his keeping it will sure preserve him" to an anonymous manuscript lapidary. Not designated in the poem is the following excerpt, partially quoted: "With the Magdalenian skeleton found at Duruthy was discovered a necklace of fifty canine teeth, three of lion and the rest of bear, most of them ornamented in some fashion. . . ."

I don't think Avicenna was ever in Cologne; it was Albertus Magnus who "found an eaglestone," but after I discovered my historical error, I liked the sound too much to change the line.

POEM FOR GERMAN PAINTERS, PAGE 11: This poem was begun by my husband, Edward Batchelder, and finished by me. I am indebted to him for much of the language, which remains from his original version.

WEB, PAGE 13: "Vowels velvet" comes from the poem "A Chain for Madelaine" by Gerald Burns.

TROPISM, PAGE 54: The following parallel observations made by Edward H. Thompson and Carl Jung were the foundation for the poem. Quotations in the poem are from the same sources. The instinctive creaturely turning-with-awe toward the source of light becomes the search for historical artifacts, buried consciousness, and spiritual growth.

I stood upon the roof of this temple one morning just as the first rays of sun reddened the distant horizon. The morning stillness was profound. All the sky above and the earth below seemed to be breathlessly waiting for something. Then the great round sun came up, flaming splendidly, and instantly the whole world sang and hummed. The birds in the trees and the insects on the ground sang a grand Te Deum. Nature herself taught primal man to be a sun worshipper and man in his heart of hearts still follows the ancient teaching.

—Edward Herbert Thompson, archaeologist, from his diary at Chichén-Itzá

I formed the habit of taking my camp stool and sitting under an umbrella acacia just before dawn. . . . Near my observation point was a high cliff inhabited by big baboons. Every morning they sat quietly, almost motionless, on the ridge of the cliff facing the sun, whereas throughout the rest of the day they ranged noisily through the forest, screeching and chattering. They reminded me of the great baboons of the temple of Abu Simbel in Egypt, which perform the gesture of adoration.

—Carl Jung, *Memories, Dreams, Reflections*